TEENS AND BUSINESS HANDBOOK

What every teen needs to know about business

and their first job

JERRY T. HANCOCK

EDITED BY JACOB C. RATLIFF

Additional copies of the book may be purchased on the website. Quantity discounts and custom/corporate training is available.

ISBN 978-0-578-62113-5
©2020 Jerry T. Hancock
All rights reserved
Published by Chartwell Press
400 Avinger Lane, #200
Davidson, NC 28036
(Additional Copies 8.95 each USD)
https://teensandbusinesshandbook.com

Acknowledgements

A lot of people have helped to make this book possible. Thanks to Jacob Ratliff for superb editing and to those who contributed their personal stories. Some of their wisdom is shared throughout the book.

Specific thanks to:

- Terry Wilson
- Tom Maupin
- Dr. John Kuykendall
- Rande Howell
- Bob McIntosh
- Curtis Charlesworth
- Frank Bragg
- Bill Cockrill
- Emmie Alexander
- Jacob Ratliff

Introduction

My first job was in a nearby small, family owned grocery store when I was only 13. It was a husband and wife operation and one or both was there almost all the time in my early days. But soon, they trusted me enough that they would leave for several days at a time when school was out. I would open and close the store (taking the cash home with me on my bike) order inventory, and make bank deposits. Because I was there with the owner and numerous other businesspeople (vendors, customers, contractors), I was exposed to a LOT of business talk. I learned quickly what was good business practice and what was not. The owner shared everything with me, including how he determined markup for the merchandise, inventory management, etc. What a treat! I quickly learned things my working friends took months to learn in their job at a supermarket or department store.

You likely will not get that kind of hands-on training on your first job. But you need much of the information, nonetheless. So, you may have to be keenly observant and ask a lot of questions in order to be successful.

You need to know, at a minimum:

- How does my job fit into the big picture?
- What is the strategy to control costs?
- What are manager's priorities?
- What things will I be measured on?

The answers to these questions will help you carry out the company's plans and find your place in the mix.

Most teens have never had the chance to learn basic business expectations and concepts or to think about career. They typically get their first job in high school or college, and then drift onto a second or third job without giving much thought to their future or career or even their developing capabilities.

Contrast that with a worker who has developed his/her own *plan* for their career, chosen a *mentor* to help in that effort, *read* extensively about business practices and the industry in which they are interested, and taken some vocational *tests* to fine tune areas of interest. The result is a very different employee.

The purpose of this book is to help teens:

- get some idea of what to expect on their first job
- define their own occupational goals and move toward a satisfying career.

My hope is that this book will help teens like you take an early interest in business and your own work future. Learning some basics will save yourself a lot of time and frustration and help you find your niche in the world of work much sooner.

Most of us did not use a formal process in deciding our respective careers. It just happened, and the results are mixed in terms of satisfaction. For some people, their first job became their career and they are very happy. But for many others, their job (career) is just a boring place to spend their time until retirement.

Once I was teaching a Time Management class in a large company. When I arrived, there was one participant already in his seat. We chatted about the topic of the training and he said, "I'll tell you my idea of time management. I hate my job, but I only have 30 years until retirement." What a waste. What a missed opportunity. What a cost to the company and a loss for the employee. Chances are, in a different situation, this person could have thrived and looked forward every day to getting to work.

That's what I want for you: A job matched to your interests and skills such that you can't wait to get to work every day and learn more about it. I've been fortunate to have had that most of my career. I hope to show you how to improve your chances of having that also.

My hope is that this book will be helpful in steering teenagers toward their chosen field (or helping them decide). That would be success.

Jerry T. Hancock

Table of Contents

Your First Job: Some Coaching

As you think about your first job or the one you're moving to, the following suggestions should be helpful:

- **Always do your best work**, not because you're being told to but because your standards are very high. Hold yourself to perfection as best you can and meet the goals of your supervisor.

- **Always arrive on time and stay a little past quitting time** to clean up and close out or turn over to the next shift. This will mark you as a dedicated employee and will bring its own reward.

- **Your attitude really matters.** Come to work with a positive attitude ready to do the job without complaints or grumbling. (If you find that hard to do, you're probably in a bad fit.)

- **Believe in yourself.** You were hired because you impressed someone that you could do the job. Prove that to them and yourself every day.

- **Ask for challenging opportunities.** Make yourself available for the unpleasant work that others choose not to do.

- **Volunteer for every opportunity you're qualified for**, especially those that do not bring extra pay. It will expand your understanding of the business and it will give you confidence that will pay off in the future.

- **Never show up late.** You're being paid to be there for a certain number of hours. Honor that commitment.

- **Avoid gossip.** Whenever you hear gossip taking place, move on to another area. Don't participate and don't repeat what you've heard.

- **Steer clear of office politics.** It is a dead end. Don't take sides in discussions about policy.

- **Never badmouth the company. They** have invested in hiring you. If you don't like the job, move on to something else. It's unethical to take an employer's money and then complain about how they are running the business. If you have suggestions, pass them along in a meeting or through other appropriate channels. Work for change rather than complaining.

- **Try to learn not only your job but other jobs as well.** This will make you more valuable to the company and will increase your efficiency and knowledge level. It will also boost your confidence because you'll learn new skills.

- **Dress appropriately.** If your job requires you to interact with the public, dress accordingly. If you do not have clothing or accessories that you need, go to Goodwill or some other thrift shop and get what you need.

- **As much as you can, help other employees do their job.** Pitch in and offer assistance if you can do so without neglecting your own job.

- **In meetings, pay attention to the flow of dialogue.** Who seems to hold the power and whose opinion seems to be dominating? Think about what you might say If you're invited to contribute. By all means if you have suggestions to improve the business, speak up confidently. Couch your suggestions in terms such as, "I know I'm the new person here, but it seems to me that ......" Do this without criticizing current procedures. Often fresh eyes see opportunities that have been overlooked.

- **Remember that your boss is not your parent** and you're no longer at home. Don't ask for special consideration. Carry your own weight and do the job well.

- **Work the hours you're assigned faithfully.** If you want extra income or experience, volunteer for extra shifts.

- **Don't ask for a different shift** except in an absolute emergency. Schedules are complicated and when you aren't available, it creates problems for others and your manager.

- **Try to think like a manager** no matter your job. Always ask yourself questions such as:

    o   Is this the most efficient way to do this process?

    o   What ideas do I have about saving money for the company?

    o   What would help us please customers more or bring in new customers?

    o   How can I better understand the requirements of my manager?

    o   What can I do to improve things around here?

o What can I do that will have the biggest positive impact for the company?

From Terry Wilson:

For job interviews:

Despite what we want to believe, clothes do make a difference. Dress appropriately.

Show up early, not on time. Drive by the day before, at the same time as the interview, so you know where you're going and how long it will take.

If you're nervous (and you will be) wash your hands with warm water and dry thoroughly so when you shake hands, they don't feel cold and clammy.

The interview is as much about you interviewing them as it is about them interviewing you. Are they a good fit for you? Come prepared. Do your homework about the company. Most importantly, what are you looking for? What is a good fit for you?

My Plan: Your First Job

What I think I do well in this area.

What I need to work on.

What I will do about it.

What You Should Expect at Work

- No matter the job, your first few hours will likely be bewildering. Even if you have had some exposure to the company, the environment may feel like chaos.

- People will be doing their jobs carrying on as usual. You may or may not get a chance to ask questions, but you should be very observant, taking in what you see as the way things get done. It's a good idea to take notes.

- Your boss will not likely take a particular interest in seeing that you're comfortable and happy. If that occurs, that is nice, but you shouldn't expect it. In some ways, the company is like a machine running smoothly, but without a lot of maintenance. Try to figure out the "machine."

- Your job will be explained to you and you may in fact have to attend some training or watch training videos or "shadow" someone. Remember that the instructions you're given are important and you'll be exposed to them only briefly. Take notes and try to understand the reasoning behind the rules and expectations. Ask questions in your orientation rather than when you're on the job on your own.

Jerry T. Hancock

- Ask questions of your supervisor, not your teammates. Asking them will distract them from doing their work. It is not their responsibility to teach you, it is your supervisor's. Besides, they might give you wrong information.

- The work environment can sometimes seem impersonal, at least until you get used to things. Folks who have worked together for a long time tend to become close and take care of one another. Just remember you're new to the organization and you'll have to learn your way around and gain others' respect.

- Keep in mind that this job is not likely to be your career, but still you should learn everything about it you can. You'll be surprised how this information will be helpful later, even in other jobs.

From Dr. John Kuykendall:

Well...I wish I'd known how to drive when they put me behind the wheel of a truck which we had carefully loaded with 30 300-pound blocks of ice that needed to be delivered all over west Charlotte! But that's another story.

I suppose the moral (if there is one) is that there is a thin line between ambition and idiocy. Be bold to identify your potential attributes for a job, but modest enough to convey your need for guidance.

My Plan: What you should expect at work

What I think I do well in this area.

What I need to work on.

What I will do about it.

Jerry T. Hancock

Business Basics You Should Know

- The first thing you need to keep in mind about any business is that it is there to make a profit. Almost every rule or regulation or procedure is based on improving the company's bottom line or keeping people safe. When you're tempted to criticize how something is done, think first about how it contributes to the bottom line.

- Every company has a "culture" and it will be important that you learn that culture. That means there are "unwritten rules," certain ways of doing things and certain beliefs and understandings that somehow get absorbed by employees. It will be to your advantage to learn the culture and perhaps compare it to other places you have been (church, school, camp).

- In most well-run businesses, people are held to goals and performance expectations. You may be in a job that requires a certain level of productivity, but even if you're not, your contribution to the company must be more than you're costing them.

- Bosses are as different as flowers in the field. Yours may be harsh and critical or kind to a fault. Regardless, the boss is the boss and for the most part you should follow instructions given to you. You'll need to figure out where your ideas and suggestions can be utilized and how to communicate them.

- In business, there is a direct relationship effort and payoff (reward). The rate of pay is based on a certain amount of effort or contribution. The way to earn more is to contribute more. Asking for more pay because you "need" it doesn't make sense to a business. But businesses will pay more for more valuable contributions/efforts.

From Tom Maupin…

When I was a teenager, I wish someone had suggested that I read "The Four Agreements." The book was written by a Toltec, Michel Ruiz. The Toltecs believed that if you make the following 4 agreements WITH YOURSELF, your life will be in balance. The 4 agreements are:

1) Be true to your word

2) Don't make assumptions

3) Don't take things personally

4) Do the best that you can

Practicing the 4 agreements should help anyone move through life with less drama.

My Plan: Business Basics

What I think I do well in this area.

What I need to work on.

What I will do about it.

What the Business Expects of You

- A business is like a smooth-running machine, it's dependent on everyone doing their job. Likely you'll be cut some slack on your first few days at work, but you should be aware that proficiency is the name of the game and you should be working hard to improve your mastery of the job.

- For the most part you'll be expected to take care of yourself, manage your breaks and lunch hours and your gear, if that is required.

- The most important expectation is attendance and punctuality. Never miss a day if you can help it. It's important to take care of yourself too and take personal time, so make sure to do so while also requesting time off well in advance.

- Being at work "on time" means being at your work station at start time—having already gotten your coffee, chatted with friends, used the bathroom. If you need to do those things, get there 5 minutes early.

- Needless to say, supplies are expensive and an important cost item for the company. Don't waste supplies and, of course, never take supplies home with you--even if you see

Jerry T. Hancock

someone else doing it. (Get in the habit of checking your pockets every day before you leave to return any gadgets or tools you may be using.)

- In almost any job, you'll be exposed to company processes and perhaps even trade secrets. You should guard these with your life and never be anything other than trustworthy. If you have any questions about what is allowed, ask your supervisor or consult your employee handbook.

Walk into a Chick-fil-A and look at their training program for teenagers. It starts with customers as guests and continues with "It's a pleasure to serve you!" and they act on it. – Rande Howell

My Plan: What the Business Expects

What I think I do well in this area.

What I need to work on.

What I will do about it.

Becoming Successful

- If you have not done so already, it is a good idea to read Stephen Covey's *Seven Habits of Highly Effective People*. Certain behaviors help people become successful. Learn from observing the positive habits of others.

- As soon as possible, find a mentor or several mentors within the organization. This will take a while since you're new but find someone with a healthy personality and who "knows the ropes." You will want to pick their brain about how to do the job but also about *life* lessons you need to learn. Invite them to lunch or breakfast off the clock—and pay for their meal!

- You can become very disciplined about working for your success just like you study for a mid-term test or a special project. Get in the habit of a laser focus on a job of interest and master it. The web has most everything you'll need.

- Work on your "people skills." Effective leaders are good at working with people and are good communicators. If you need work in this area, add it to your personal plan with deadlines by which you'll get better at it. Then find someone who will help you offline.

- One of the things I find most lacking in young people is the assertiveness to ask confidently for what they want/need to do the job. If that is an issue for you, work on it consistently, asking for feedback along the way.

- Speaking of feedback, ask for it often. It's a gift if someone offers it and it will help you grow on the job. Don't be defensive, no matter what is said. Just say, "Thanks for that."

- Set personal goals (write them down) with specific targets to hit by a certain date. Review progress regularly When you achieve them, set new goals.

- Maintain relationships. The relationships you'll form are important, even after one or both of you move on. Keep in touch with people you appreciate. Build your network. Keep contact information up to date.

- Keep in mind: Helping others is a great way to build relationships.

Jerry T. Hancock

My Plan: Being Successful

What I think I do well in this area.

What I need to work on.

What I will do about it.

Presenting Yourself: Your "Brand"

- While you'll be likely working for someone else on your first job, you should be thinking of yourself as a brand in itself. So instead of thinking of yourself as John Doe working for McDonald's, think of yourself as John Doe, Inc. (a supplier of labor) who happens to be selling his services to McDonald's for the moment. This helps you keep your value in perspective.

- If you have not done so already, you probably should attempt to secure your domain name (johndoe.com). Then add an email address that matches (john@johndoe.com). To do this, you'll need to go to a hosting service such as GoDaddy or SiteGround and find out if your name domain is available. If you purchase a year of hosting ($4 or $5 a month) they will likely give you the domain free and the email as well. You can also build a personal website. (Get the parents involved since this is a contract.)

- Your good name is your brand. Your "brand" is golden. Protect it with all you've got. Don't let your name get sullied by getting in trouble or tarnishing it with gossip or bad behavior.

- Earn your good reputation by

  o Doing what you say you'll do; being dependable

- o Taking initiative—notice what needs to be done and do it.
- o Pitching in, helping others out
- o Focusing on the details: follow up and follow through

- Because you're a brand yourself, you should always be thinking ahead of what's next for the brand. There is a section on career planning later. Read it carefully and start a notebook or electronic file to keep notes and plans.

My Plan: Presenting Yourself (Brand)

What I think I do well in this area.

What I need to work on.

What I will do about it.

Job vs. Career

- Do you think of your job as a career? It's likely too early for that. You'll probably have a number of jobs before you settle on a career. But nonetheless, you should be thinking always about where this job is leading. If it's just a job for the moment, learn everything you can about it and the industry. You'll be surprised that you'll be able to use that information later.

- You should try to make your first job one that is fun for you. Do you have technical skills that might get you in the door at a tech firm? That would be awesome. So, make a real effort to match your interests with your job. If you can't do that immediately, keep that as a goal.

- Listen to your gut about how excited you are about any given job. If you hate it, you'll never do your best. But if you LOVE it, you'd almost do it for free! You can't wait to get there every day.

- Your first job may not have a lot of potential—but don't undersell it. If it is with a sizeable company, there are numerous other opportunities in the company which might interest you. Who knows, you might stay with that company forever, ending up as its president!

- In every job you have, constantly ask yourself: What am I learning? How can I use what I'm learning in my current job? How can I use what I'm learning in future jobs?

- Throughout this book, we have suggested you be assertive about getting what you want in a job. Make your goals known to the appropriate people, but also do such a good job that your superiors are already thinking of where you might be placed next.

- In earlier times, it was common to stay in the same job for decades. Not so anymore. People move around more, usually for higher pay or more challenging responsibilities or to get away from a bad supervisor. Keep your resume up to date, adding any new responsibilities you have been given or awards you have earned, especially things you have volunteered for.

- Also, remember sometimes a lateral move is just what you need to learn new skills (or work with different people).

My Plan: Job vs. Career

What I think I do well in this area.

What I need to work on.

What I will do about it.

Planning Your Future: Your personal plan

- There are numerous websites to help you with developing your career plan. They have a lot of things in common, such as: personal goals, salary goals, promotions, etc. We'll put a simple plan in the Resource section.

- A good place to keep your career plan is on your phone or PC where you can update it easily. Add dates by which you'll reach goals. Include earning goals and other measurable metrics. Example: I will be making $xxxx by December 31 of this year.

- It might seem a bit much to put together a career plan when your hope is to just get a job. But writing down goals has a way of making them happen, so you should always be aspiring to be better next month, next year. Some people post their goals on the dresser mirror so they are reminded of them constantly.

- If you're not sure where you'd be best suited, get some books or read some articles and visit some websites about the business or job you're interested in. Learn all you can about it and don't just focus on the salary. Your happiness is equally important and if you don't *enjoy* the job, you'll be miserable.

Jerry T. Hancock

- Ask around to see who is in the kind of work you find appealing. If possible, ask to meet with them and have some well thought out questions to ask. Don't be shy about this. My experience is that most people are gracious and enjoy talking about their work and accomplishments. They might be a conduit for you getting a job in their company or industry.

From Frank Bragg:

I have lots of personal experience as I had 13 jobs as a youngster before college. And I have mentored all 15 grandkids with their jobs... they also learn to answer the question "Why should I hire you?"

My Plan: Planning your Future

What I think I do well in this area.

What I need to work on.

What I will do about it.

College or Not?

- In 2018, the Bureau of Labor Statistics reported that 69.1 percent of students who graduated high school in 2016 were enrolled in college. About 49 percent of these students are enrolled in community colleges, according to a 2017 report issued by the National Student Clearinghouse Research Center.

- The question as to whether to go to college is a real one. What do you want to do for a living? Teach school, work in an office, modify cars for racing? The answer to that question should drive your decision. And be sure to involve your guidance counselor, your parents and other adults you respect in your decision.

- Keep in mind that very few decisions are irrevocable. If you decide to go to college after a year working, that's fine. Just don't get tempted to skip college and keep working--not without a lot of thought.

- It used to be a given that a college degree meant tons more income over a lifetime. However, the technology boom has changed that. Many technical workers make more than their college-educated friends, but that is not a given. And there are more options available generally today.

- If you do go to college, be among the 40% who finish in 4 years. And try to discern what your vocation is going to be by the end of your sophomore year.

- To make a smart decision, make a list of the 5 or 6 vocations that interest you then research the education requirements for each. Also research the average salary for each (not just starting salary). If money is your driving issue, you need to know what income to expect.

- It is certainly normal to not have a clue what you want to do for a living when you're in high school. You should not feel bad about that. But there are tests and instruments which will help you learn what you might be good at.

- The bottom line is you should do what makes you happy without feeling pressure from parents or others. Plenty of artistic people are very happy practicing their craft and not making a lot of money. Just actively consider the trade-offs.

- Remember, you're never too old to go back to college.

Jerry T. Hancock

Overcoming Your Fears

- This is your work: **get over your fears**. FEAR stands for false evidence appearing real. Most of your fears are unfounded and will never happen. But if you allow it, fear will take over your life—and certainly your new job. (See the section on self-confidence.)

- What is your fear based on? Fear of embarrassment? Lack of skill? Making a mistake? Saying something stupid? Doing something stupid? If you're honest with yourself, the chances of those things happening are minimal. And consider this: Because you're new, you may get a free pass on making mistakes.

- YOU are the only person who can work on this issue. Make up your mind to get past your fears. Get a mentor to help you. Talk to your parents—yes, your parents. They likely have some good ideas on this since they have experienced this.

- If you need to take this slowly, make small steps at first, then increase the risk. Do things that are uncomfortable for you. It helps you grow and become a leader. There is no reason to let fear hold you back or keep you from giving your best to the world. There are resources on the web which can help.

- **Presentations**: most people are very nervous about making a presentation. Even speaking up at a meeting or sharing information with a group can give some of us the willies. Again, work hard on this. Practice in front of a mirror or with siblings or family, or even the dog. *If you know the subject, you should have no problem doing a presentation about it*. Whether it is with one other person or an auditorium full of people, the approach is the same: Be yourself, show interest in the audience by making eye contact, speak a little louder and more enthusiastically than normal and you'll be fine. Remember, the audience is sympathetic. They want you to do well. Again, resources are on the web.

- **We all have self-doubt.** You may doubt yourself because of your lack of experience in life. It is helpful to know that we all have some of this and actually it is a good thing because it keeps us on our toes doing our best. The trick is to keep working on this. You are valuable. You have talents and gifts. The world needs what you have to offer! You may feel like you're a big fake and not what you seem, but that's coming from your doubtful side. Tame it. Don't let it ruin your life. Do lots of self-talk such as "I can do this," "I have a skill that others may not have" etc.

Jerry T. Hancock

My Plan: Overcoming your fears

What I think I do well in this area.

What I need to work on.

What I will do about it.

Developing Self-confidence

- You probably won't feel very confident your first days on the job. There's so much to learn and you may feel inadequate. But confidence comes from success and each day you'll build on your success and quickly become more confident. You can speed up this process by asking a lot of questions and taking on challenging assignments.

- Self-confidence is more than a psychological term. It comes from trust in yourself and an awareness that you have capabilities that have value. Trust your judgment, even in the early days. Believing in your own hunches can go a long way toward building self-confidence, especially when you turn out to be right.

- Experience is the greatest teacher of self-confidence. The more you observe and try to learn and understand the job, the more confident you'll get in making suggestions about processes and procedures. Give yourself a talk each day before work saying things like, "I have a lot of skills and I can do this job."

Jerry T. Hancock

- The negative side of confidence is the possibility of being too critical of yourself. When you start putting yourself down or criticizing your own ideas, make a note of it and stop that behavior. This is self-defeating and will interfere with your success for the rest of your career. Don't do it!

- Nobody is born with confidence. We all have to learn it. And one way we learn it is to "fake" it. Fake it till you make it. That does not mean you should be disingenuous. It means *acting* confident, which makes you *be* more confident. Sounds weird, huh. But it works. Show the traits of confidence: look people in the eye, speak with enthusiasm and good volume, have a firm handshake, show interest in others. If you're an introvert, this may be harder. But give it a try. It works! This is critical if you have a job interacting with the public. Be friendly, upbeat. Make eye contact. Show some excitement and act like you're glad to see this customer/person/colleague.

- Finally, actively study people you perceive to be confident. What are they doing that makes you feel that way about them? What traits do you want to emulate? If you know one of those people well, it might be worth having a chat with them about this subject.

My Plan: Developing Self Confidence

What I think I do well in this area.

What I need to work on.

What I will do about it.

Getting Noticed by Your Boss

- There is a story about a construction site in which one worker always wore a red shirt. When he was asked why, he said he wanted to make sure the boss knew that he was on the job and working hard. It was his idea of making sure he was noticed by standing out from the crowd.

- The most important thing you can do as a new hire is to do your job, then offer to help out in ways that go outside your job description. But keep in mind this is only a good idea if your job is taken care of. Otherwise you might be accused of meddling.

- Managers are always looking for new ideas and creative ways to improve efficiency and save money. It's worth your time to spend a few minutes at the end of the day thinking about what you have seen and where efficiencies can be improved. Since you're new, you won't be bound by the traditional arguments about why something can't be done. Take advantage of that position and offer your good ideas.

- You'll encounter people on the job who are simply filling the space and want to do as little as possible. You'll want to avoid these people and make sure your work output is beyond what is expected. This is a business and you're offering a service that costs money (your time). The return on investment means that you're productive and giving back to the company more than they are investing in you.

- The negative way to get noticed by the boss is to complain or to call attention to yourself.

- Doing good work will bring recognition as will helping out in a jam or volunteering for unpleasant tasks. Make yourself available but don't come across as a know it all.

Jerry T. Hancock

My Plan: Getting Noticed by Your Boss

What I think I do well in this area.

What I need to work on.

What I will do about it.

What Teamwork Means

- Making the transition from working as an individual contributor to a team member is difficult for some people. As an individual, you want credit for your own ideas and you're mostly out to take care of yourself. But in the team, it is the whole team that wins, not individuals. If you have played team sports, you get this. Giving up some of your ego and sharing the credit will be important.

- Teamwork also implies that you collaborate with others as you work. This builds trust and confidence in the team and shows that you're not self-centered and pursuing your own agenda. In teamwork, you learn that everybody has a role to play and something to contribute.

- Should you get a chance to lead a team, you'll want to make sure you hear from everyone on the team. There is no "I" in team as they say.

- Conflict is present everywhere and will certainly be present on a team. Learning how to navigate conflicting ideas or personalities will be important. You may be exposed to people aggressively defending their own position. In a successful team, conflict management is seen as an important skill and one that everybody needs to learn. You might want to find some resources about this.

- Another unique concept of teamwork is that everybody's opinion counts  equally. If you're in a meeting and notice that someone has not spoken up, it might be a good idea to ask the person directly for their thoughts. This sets you apart as a collaborator and it helps to make sure everybody's fingerprints are on the final decision.

- It may seem that you don't have much influence as a beginning worker. But in a team, good ideas are priceless. If the team is functioning properly, your ideas will be received and appreciated. If they are put down or criticized, you might come to believe the team is dysfunctional. Don't give up. Always advocate for an idea you believe in.

My Plan: What Teamwork Means

What I think I do well in this area.

What I need to work on.

What I will do about it.

Jerry T. Hancock

A job is much more than a place to make money. It is another "life" for you as a person. It is your new "work life" or "career," as you want to define it. You may not have the most glorious, glamorous, prestigious, red carpet job in the world ... but you do have the most important job in the world ... yours! It is "your" job, position, career, etc. Make it yours. It is your mark, your witness, make it your calling, for however long you have it.

Go at it like it is your gift to humanity. You will interact with people every day. Make it your ministry to make the lives of the people with whom you work a little better. You never know when yours is the only smile or pleasant voice that person might hear. You never know when you have been strategically placed to make a difference in someone's life. Do you want it to be a positive or a negative difference? The beauty lies in that the choice is strictly up to you. Which will it be?

What I am suggesting is not easy. It is not our "natural inclination." Some days you'll be tired, you'll have life's burdens on you like everyone else. Some days you'll only want to do your job and go home. Stress will come into your work life just like it is in your personal life. You will not feel motivated to help others and be the bright spot in their lives when you cannot see the bright in your own life. You will have to choose which way you go. It simply MUST be a conscious choice. Choose to make it ... and make it in the right direction.

Much like the Native American legend of the two wolves that are at constant battle within each of us. One is light and wants to do right by others; one is dark and is only out to serve itself. Their battle is constant, always at each other's throats. "Which one wins?" asks the young brave. The wise chief responds, "The one I feed." Feed the right wolf in your work, but you have to feed it – the feeding does not come without decision to do so. It will spill over into your personal life as well.

Robert G. McIntosh

Using What You Learn

- The first few days of the new job will provide a ton of information. You'll be learning details of the job, but you'll also hear a lot about the culture of the company and individual people you'll be working with. Absorb as much of this as you can and file it away in your mind to be used later.

- Learning the particulars of the job is only a small fraction of what you'll be expected to do. Learning the *hows* and *whys* of getting things done is equally important. When someone shares with you a reason why something is done in a particular way, question that but also be prepared to follow their lead. The next step is to pass that on to other new workers.

- One of the facts of business life is that what you learned yesterday will come in useful today. Even when it seems irrelevant, things you learn on the job provide experience that you'll call on later. This is why an experienced manager is valuable. Not only does he or she know how to avoid calamity, they make better decisions because of what they have witnessed in the past.

- Just because you're new does not mean that you can't offer a lot of suggestions for the company. Your fresh eyes will see things that others may have overlooked. Think about how to pass along that information in a positive way. If you have a trusted cohort, run the idea past that person before presenting it to your boss or in a team meeting.

- Experience is valuable in the workplace because lessons learned by making mistakes stay with you. And they become a sieve through which you filter options when you encounter the next problem. Experience transfers to other jobs as well which is why an executive in an automobile business can do a great job in the food business. It is the problem-solving skill that matters.

My Plan: Using What You Learn

What I think I do well in this area.

What I need to work on.

What I will do about it.

From Curtis Charlesworth:

1) Put your cellphone away. An employer is paying you to work not be on your phone.

2) Don't expect to be the CEO in two years. Progression should be gradual and, in some cases, lateral so you can be better prepared when advancement opportunities present themselves.

3) Work. I've seen so many young people do as little as humanly possible in their jobs. It's as if they seem entitled to a paycheck because they show up.

4) Show up to work on time every day. A job isn't there for you to show up when you feel like it or have nothing else to do that day.

5) Constructive criticism isn't demeaning; it is to help you improve.

6) Be observant. What can you learn from your boss or colleagues? How can you serve your customers better by anticipating their needs?

7) You don't need to blurt out every thought that enters your brain. Use discretion. Anticipate how your comments will be received.

Helping Others Succeed

- One of the hallmarks of successful people is that they are willing to help others succeed as well. This is a *decision* they have made to always try to help others. It is an attitude that you should adopt as you as you start your career.

- The concept of working as a team may be new to first-time workers. The tendency is to take care of ourselves and assume that others will do the same. However, teamwork is intended to help everyone succeed and share the credit. No one succeeds unless everyone succeeds.

- In the early days of a new job, you'll be very appreciative of people who help you out. Not just in showing you the job, but also in teaching you the expectations of the company and details about the work environment. You'll want to make sure you pass that on to others.

- One way you can help others succeed is to be a good listener. As your career advances, you'll run into opportunities to hear people's frustration with the job or their concerns about specific elements of the job. Being a good listener marks you as a caring person. There are specific techniques that indicate you're listening. The one we most often fail to use is paraphrasing back what we have heard in our own words. This is a great technique to learn and use in almost every business and personal environment. (I have written a book *(having) Better Conversations*, available on Amazon.)

- You're also helping others succeed when you volunteer for jobs that others may not want to do. It's a positive indication that you're putting the team interest ahead of your own and it also gives you experience that you would not otherwise get.

- Helping others succeed is an excellent way to build lasting relationships since you now have something in common.

- Finally, don't worry about who gets the credit. A basketball player who sets up the shot is as valuable as the player who puts it through the net.

Jerry T. Hancock

My Plan: Helping Others Succeed

What I think I do well in this area.

What I need to work on.

What I will do about it.

Behaviors to Avoid

You probably already know this list, but here goes:

- Negativity (it is contagious)
- Gossip (it hurts others)
- Badmouthing the company (you look small)
- Complaining about the job or the company
- Goofing off
- Watching the clock
- Appearing uninterested
- Showing up late or leaving early
- Being unprepared for work
- Poor hygiene
- Dressing inappropriately
- Jokes or comments that are in poor taste
- Sharing too much about your personal life
- Failing to show enthusiasm for the customer
- Arguing with others, including customers
- Being defensive about feedback
- Ignoring customer or supervisor requests
- Wearing too much cologne or perfume
- Acting like you can't wait to get off work
- Complaining about overtime or work demands
- Returning late from breaks or lunch
- Not being on the job at designated start time
- Not responding to calls or messages
- Taking *anything* from the company
- Trying to buddy up with your supervisor
- Making excuses for poor performance
- Not appreciating the job and the company

My Plan: Behaviors to Avoid

What I think I do well in this area.

What I need to work on.

What I will do about it.

First Job Advice from Bill Cockrill

1. Every job offers opportunities to learn and grow, not just in the specific skills that the job requires, but in such general areas as how to cooperate with fellow workers, how to relate to those customers and others outside the realm of your employer, how to pace yourself and become more efficient and reliable.

2. Try to understand what the goals or mission of your employer are, and how your specific job relates to that larger purpose.

3. Remember that others are depending on your doing your job well so that they can do theirs well. You are not competitors but colleagues.

4. Consider how your behavior outside of work time reflects on your employer.

5. Be honest in all that you do. If your job requires or implies that you need to be dishonest, find another job.

6. If everything about your job is not enjoyable, remember that if it were all fun, they would not be paying you to do it. Nevertheless, relish those parts that are enjoyable and nurture positive relationships with your co-workers, customers and clients.

7. Do not pursue wealth so much as competence and integrity, as well as satisfaction in accomplishment.

Jerry T. Hancock

When to Move On

There will come a time when you decide it is time to move on. That may come early on the job or after years in your career.

How will you know when it is time to leave? Here are some signals:

- The environment has become toxic, unhealthy

- Too much focus on personalities and not performance

- Poor performance gets ignored or rewarded

- Your supervisor is a jerk or unfair or inept

- There is little or nothing left to learn on this job

- You find yourself coasting through the day

- The work is no longer challenging

- You dread coming to work

- You're not fairly compensated

- You get no credit for extraordinary effort

Are You an Entrepreneur?

- What if you cannot stand the possibility of working for someone else? What if you feel you're smarter than most of the bosses you might work for? What if you're just teeming with ideas and are always looking for a chance to implement them? What if you have a huge thirst for how things work? What if you like starting a project from nothing, finishing it, then moving on to another? **You might just be an entrepreneur.**

- Entrepreneurs thrive on challenges. They like to take on the impossible and make it work. They have a lot of regard for their own capabilities and are willing to risk failure in order to achieve success. Sometimes they are driven by financial motives, but more often they just like "the thrill of the hunt."

- Entrepreneurs like inventions, innovation, new ways of doing things. They are rarely happy with the status quo and as a result they are often troublemakers when placed in a tightly controlled organization. What inspires them (freedom) is usually simply not allowed. Their ideas are stifled and often they are told "We've never done it that way."

Jerry T. Hancock

- Entrepreneurs have little patience for naysayers and people who can't think creatively. They assume that everyone can see the obvious things they are seeing so why continue doing business the old way?

- If the descriptions above seem to fit you, you might have a rough road ahead if you go to work for a traditional company. You may have no other choice, but your instincts will be telling you there has to be a better way. And as you try to persuade people of that better way, you can create some ripples within the company. If you believe you're cut out to be an entrepreneur, an independent thinker who would rather have a successful project than a raise, you might want to work toward a different kind of job. It is possible you may find an entry level job that rewards entrepreneurial thinking, but not likely. Most of us start out following the traditional methods already in place without much questioning. Entrepreneurs find that hypocritical, not to mention boring.

- You may enjoy working for a small, but fast-growing company where you'll have an opportunity to try new things and grow with the company.

- If you have this ability to see what others cannot, a restlessness about creating something from scratch, a confidence that you're the one to do it, and a willingness to give up creature comforts to see your ideas succeed -- you may be much happier in a creative, entrepreneurial role. Many entrepreneurs make far less money than they could make at other jobs but detest the idea of giving up their autonomy for the sake of a paycheck.

- It's worth it to take a hard look at yourself and see whether a routine job will make you happy. Or whether you can tolerate such a job while you quietly work toward something more exciting and creative. Good luck!

- If you're convinced you want to be your own boss, figure out a way to start small—maybe as a hobby. Figure a way to fund it (parents, friends, selling off some toys) then go for it. But do some research to see who is already in that market.

Jerry T. Hancock

My Plan: Are You an Entrepreneur?

What I think I do well in this area.

What I need to work on.

What I will do about it.

From a frustrated boss (anonymous)

1. When you're given a task:

   - Make sure you understand the big picture goal. Knowledge jobs are not an assembly line / linear process. Your job is not to do exactly what you're told and no more -- it is to help your manager and the organization achieve their goals. If you run into a barrier, think about possible solutions and present those to your manager.

     Example: You're asked to have lunch delivered for a noon meeting in two days. You and your manager consider restaurant options and pick A. At 12:10, your manager calls from the meeting and asks where lunch is. You reply that A did not open until 11 so got the order late and it should be delivered by 12:45. Your manager is thinking:
     1) I am embarrassed in front of a room full of people because we dropped the ball on something simple.
     2) We chose A two days ago. Why didn't you put the order in immediately instead of waiting until this morning?
     3) Really wish you had let me know about the problem. We could have just ordered pizza.

4) You knew this was a one-hour meeting. Do I really need to tell a college graduate that delivery time is more important than restaurant choice?

- o Make sure you have a deadline for having it completed. If you're having trouble meeting a deadline, talk with your manager in advance and ask for priorities.

- o After you complete a task, ask for feedback on what went well and what could have been better. Even if you aren't in school, the most important thing for you to do right now is to learn!

2. It is ALWAYS okay to ask questions – and not just okay, but a smart thing to do. Your manager would rather help you get started the right way than send you back to re-do work.

3. No job is 9-5, M-F. Just as you sometimes need to flex your schedule, for personal appointments, for instance, there are times when the organization needs for you to flex your schedule. You should be compensated for your time, but don't say it "isn't fair" for you to be asked to work differently because you don't make the big bucks.

4. Occasionally everyone needs to take a day off for mental health, and that's OK. Just know that when you're out, there are real consequences

for other people and their ability to complete their work. Take a day when you need it, but don't do it often. Your manager and your coworkers will start to resent you if they regularly have to pick up your work. (Of course, if you're really ill that is different. But you can't take two days off every month because your period is heavy, snowflake.)

5. Proof. Your. Work. Use spellcheck. Make sure you have dates/times/data correct. This isn't school and I am not a teacher who will let you slide until the final draft. We should be taking your work to the next level, not doing remedial proofing.

6. If you have nothing to do, ask your manager and coworkers if you can do anything to help them. Show your value.

7. If you find that you don't want to go in to work, that probably means you need to find another job. This doesn't necessarily mean that you're wrong or the organization is bad. It means this just isn't a good fit.

Jerry T. Hancock

Resource A: Interviewing

Before the interview

- Best advice: Dress like you're going to church. Even if the job environment is very informal, you'll be better off to overdress than underdress. Your dress is some indicator of your maturity level.

- Pay particular attention to your shoes. No tennis shoes or worn-looking loafers. If you must, go to Goodwill and buy shoes just for this occasion.

- It should go without saying, but.....
  No tank tops, jeans or shorts and keep cologne and perfumes, makeup, and jewelry to a minimum. And, women, no low-cut tops or short skirts.

- Be sure to take a resume and references in case you're asked. On your resume, count every experience you have had which might apply.

- Learn everything you can about the company and the job before you go. Scour the website.

- Think up every question you might be asked, but be prepared for unexpected questions like:
  Tell me about a time when you really had to solve a problem fast.

What do you do to keep yourself informed about the news?

Talk about your plans for your 10 year anniversary on the job.

What will your references likely say about you?

During the interview

- Try to illustrate your social maturity and awareness by sitting upright, looking poised and confident and making eye contact.

- Keep your answers short. Let the interviewer ask for details. Don't ramble on.

- Speak clearly and confidently. Look the interviewer in the eye. And smile. Don't trail off to nothingness with your answers. It is ok to take a few seconds to compose your answer.

- Highlight your strengths and how they might fit this job.

- Try to weave into your answers specific things you have learned as an intern or on school projects or even at summer camp. Life experiences count!

Jerry T. Hancock

- Take notes to think about later. Also, on your notepad have some questions you'll want to get answered.

After the interview

- When the interview is finished, ask when you might follow up (unless that question has already been answered, of course).

- If you have no luck with getting a traditional job, sit down and make a list of services you can provide for a fee, ranging from dog sitter to tutoring. (There's a bunch on the web.)

- Send a handwritten thank you note *and* a brief thank you email as soon as you get home.

Resource B: Developing a Career Plan

A career plan is nothing more than a guide to planning your future. It should have most of these ingredients:

1. Some assessment of the kind of work you would like to do. Include your interests, talents, skills.

2. Your plan for exploration; how you'll go about your career planning (web searches, interviews with people in the business, reading).

3. Your elimination process, deciding on a fit. (What will be your criteria for deleting a job?)

4. What are your goals for income, job stability, travel, benefits, promotions, etc.

5. What is your plan of attack? (How many resumes you'll send out, appointments you'll set up, etc.)

Jerry T. Hancock

Resource C: Job Search

- Before you start searching, sit down and make a list of the types of jobs you might enjoy or be good at. Start there.

- Your first search should be with friends and family or teachers who already know you. They might know of a job or someone to talk to. It is always better when you have a referral (John Doe said I should talk to you about….)

- Are you on social media? Make it known you are looking. Network through other church/family/friend/relative/teacher contacts also. Having an up-to-date LinkedIn profile is a must.

- Suggest yourself as an intern to a company you're interested in. You can find many of the company's managers on their website. (If you find someone's email, you can likely use that format to figure out someone else's whose email might be missing.)

- Don't just consider traditional employers. Consider small companies if they fit your search profile.

- For any job, but especially where you'll have customer contact, practice your smile and pleasant conversation. You might have to work at this.

Resource D: Call Log

(to keep up with calls/appointments)

Name/ Company	Date called	Results/ notes?	Follow-up date

Jerry T. Hancock

Resource E: Selecting/Using a Mentor

If you wish to establish a mentor relationship with someone, here are a few suggestions:

- The person need not be at your place of employment. It can be a trusted family friend, or another business connection.
- The mentor should be of the same gender as you to keep things simple.
- Don't be in a rush. Find someone who seems to be compatible with your personality.
- Know what you want from this person. Company knowledge? Job knowledge? Success pointers?
- Be assertive about asking for what you need from this person. Don't assume they will know.
- Keep a notebook of well thought out questions and notes from your meetings.
- Don't ask questions you should take responsibility for learning yourself.
- Set a regular default meeting time.
- Remember this person is doing you a favor. Thank them.
- Respect their time and never be late. They have a job to do.
- Ask about their route to success, try to understand their values/priorities.
- Commit to mentoring others some day.
- Search the web for more ideas about making this relationship successful.

Closing Thoughts

- Starting your first job is a big deal. It not only represents a chance to earn some money, it is a definite statement of growing independence from parents and family. It is both scary and exhilarating. Enjoy!

- You'll make mistakes, but they won't be fatal. Show courage and confidence (even if you don't feel it yet).

- No matter how long your career lasts, you'll always remember your first job and the feelings associated with it. Make the most of it. Make some pictures as a keepsake.

- Take notice of what your supervisor does right and all of your future supervisors as well. Pick the best behaviors you see and create a composite model of what you want in a manager. Then be that person as your career matures.

- Finally, always help the person a few steps down the ladder. It is the right thing to do.

- Good luck! Let me hear of your success!

Jerry T. Hancock

About the Author

 Jerry Hancock is a business consultant and personal coach who has spent most of his adult life in communications, ranging from television host to advertising/communications executive. He is a partner in the consulting firm of AlexanderHancock Associates, a training and consulting company he and his wife, Emmie, founded in 1990. Since then, the company has trained thousands of people on the techniques discussed in this book through hands-on workshops. www.alexanderhancock.com

Jerry is also Executive Director of Men in Balance[tm] a nonprofit organization dedicated to the spiritual development of men and to healthy relationships. He has counseled hundreds of men and couples in Couples Communication classes. www.meninbalance.org

He is also the author of *10 Lessons for Men and How Our Partners Can Help* and *Having Better Conversations* (available on Amazon or through the author.)

Email him at jerry@jerryhancock.com

Go to the website for updates, supplemental articles and see others' comments on the blog.

Website: https://teensandbusinesshandbook.com

Additional copies of the book may be purchased on the website. Quantity discounts and custom/corporate trainings are available.

Notes

Jerry T. Hancock

Notes